Cocktails for Drivers

100-Proof Pleasure

D1314210

Contents

Fundamentals

Recipes

Appendix

Non-Alcoholic Drinks — Pure Flavor, Pure Pleasure

Your doctor recommends at least five servings of fruits and vegetables a day. Tell the truth though—how often do you hit that mark? So what could be better than slurping down a delicious cold drink filled with vitamins and minerals as a snack or even for breakfast? Surprise your family and guests with fruity smoothies, shakes, mixed drinks, and punches that even children can enjoy.

Diversity in Drinks — from Milkshakes to Punch

When preparing non-alcoholic drinks, give your imagination free reign to create unique combinations from the best ingredients.

1 | Fruit-based drinks

Any fruit that can be finely chopped with a countertop or hand blender can be used in fruit drinks. Berries, apricots, peaches, nectarines, plums, and grapes are all perfect. You don't even have to peel these fruits, just wash them! There are lots of vitamins just under the skin and the peel provides essential fiber. For grape juice, use the seedless types. Of course you'll have to peel the obvious fruit; melons, bananas, mangos, and papayas.

Don't be afraid to use store-bought juices in your drinks. Try to buy 100% pure juice whenever possible to stay away from unnecessary sugar and flavorings.

2 | Vegetable-based drinks

Any vegetable that can be eaten raw is also suitable for vegetable drinks. If you really love mixed vegetable drinks, you should purchase a juicer since few vegetables are so soft that they can easily be puréed. Good vegetables for blending include cucumbers, peeled tomatoes, radishes, and avocados. Other vegetables such as carrots, beets, and celery can be purchased in juice form.

3 | Milkshakes

With a milkshake, you can kill two birds with one stone. They provide you with both fruit and dairy (and you don't have to limit this to ordinary cow's milk—you can also use yogurt or buttermilk) so your body also gets its supply of calcium.

4 | Smoothies

A smoothie is a thick drink made from fruit or vegetables. Its consistency comes from processing frozen fruit or fresh fruit and ice cubes in a blender.

5 | Fruit mixers

For these drinks, use fresh fruits that are easily puréed, then whisk them with fresh-squeezed juices such as orange or grapefruit. Processed juices and syrups can also be added.

6 | Punches

In the case of punches, fresh fruit is puréed and then steeped with an aromatic additive such as herbs or syrup. You then add ice-cold tea or a carbonated beverage such as tonic water.

Basic Recipe and Variations

Black Tea

Prepare tea from 2 tbs tea leaves and about 1¼ cups water.

 Variations

— Lime iced tea: Sweeten tea to taste. Cut 1 lime into thin slices and place in a pitcher with lots of ice cubes. Pour tea over the top, add ½ cup ginger ale, and stir.

— Mint tea: Using a spoon, lightly crush 2 sprigs of fresh mint with sugar to taste. Strain freshly brewed tea over the top and steep for 3 minutes.

— Spiced tea: Bring 1¼ cups of water to a boil with ½ cinnamon stick, 1 tsp cardamom, and 2 whole cloves. Steep for 15 minutes, sweeten with honey, add ¾ cup milk, and bring to a boil. Stir in 2 tsp tea leaves, steep for 4 minutes, and pour through a strainer.

Coffee

Brew coffee from 4 tsp coffee grounds and 2 cups water.

Variations

— Middle-Eastern coffee: Add 1 pinch cinnamon or a little ground cardamom to the coffee grounds and brew normally. Allspice, nutmeg, and star anise also go well with coffee.

— Iced Coffee Float: Brew fresh coffee, sweeten to taste, let cool, and then refrigerate. Fill two tall glasses with 1 scoop vanilla ice cream and coffee. Garnish with whipped cream.

— Caramel coffee: Brew fresh coffee. Pour 1 tsp caramel syrup into a mug of coffee. Stir in more caramel as desired and add hot milk.

Chocolate

Combine a little milk, 2 tsp cocoa powder, and 1 tsp sugar. Using a wire whisk, stir into 1½ cups boiling milk.

Variations

— Vanilla chocolate: Slit open 1 vanilla bean and scrape out the tiny seeds. Bring 1¼ cups milk to a boil with the seeds and bean. Using a wire whisk, stir in 2 tsp cocoa powder. Season with ½ tsp cinnamon and 1 pinch chili powder. Sweeten as desired and top with whipped cream.

— Deluxe chocolate: Melt ⅓ cup semisweet chocolate chips in ¾ cup milk and 3 tbs whipping cream. Flavor with ½ tsp vanilla and sweeten as desired with sugar. Serve with whipped cream garnished with chocolate shavings.

Essential Tools for Mixing Fun

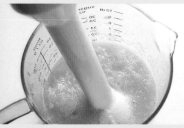

For squeezing

A citrus juicer is an absolute must. It's best to purchase one with two cones, a smaller one for lemons and limes and a larger one for oranges and grapefruit. For larger amounts an electric citrus juicer is recommended.

For Puréeing

A hand-held blender (also called a stick blender) is an easy way to purée fruit and certain types of vegetables until creamy. It's best to place the ingredients in a tall measuring cup. Then you can measure the amounts of liquid while you add them and prevent splattering when you blend.

Countertop blender

You need a powerful blender with at least 400 watts of power, especially if you're making smoothies, because these require chopping frozen fruit or ice cubes to make the drink nice and creamy. You can also use it to prepare any of the mixed drink recipes.

Ice cubes

Ice cube trays can also be used for freezing puréed fruit depending on the season. You can then use the cubes as needed. Make crushed ice in a small hand-cranked ice crusher or put the ice cubes in a tear-proof freezer bag and crush them with a hammer.

Glasses

The servings in the recipes that follow are intended to fill two tall glasses with a capacity of 1 cup. In the case of ice-cold drinks, the glasses will look nice and frosty if you dampen them and leave them in the freezer for 1 hour.

Mixing like a pro

Some drinks, such as those made from squeezed citrus juices, will be more elegant if you pour them through a fine-meshed strainer. Small spiral whisks available in specialty stores are ideal for whisking sugar or spices.

Dairy Products

Cow's milk
In addition to calcium for building bones, milk is loaded with vitamin B2. Whether you use whole milk or low-fat is up to you. The low-fat types of cow's milk contain just as many minerals as whole milk and their fat content is still sufficient to transport the vitamins.

Buttermilk
Made by processing cream into butter. With a fat content of 0.3 to 1%, it is extremely low-fat, promotes digestion, and should be stored in a cool, dark place.

Sour milk
This milk variant is produced by adding lactic acid bacteria to milk. It's fat content depends on the type of milk used.

Yogurt
Yogurt is made by adding pure cultures to pasteurized milk. It's fat content ranges from 0.3% to 10%.

Kefir
Originating in the Caucasus Mountains, kefir is now made from a fermented cow's milk. It is similar to yogurt in it's slightly sour taste, but is sold as a liquid. It is available in health and nutrition stores.

Soy milk
This vegetable milk is made from cooked, ground soybeans. It contains more iron than cow's milk, is low-fat, and cholesterol-free. It is now available in many supermarkets and is an ideal source of calcium for anyone who has difficulties with cow's milk due to lactose intolerance.

Garnishing
Made Easy

To make all of your drinks look as good as they taste, lace small garnishes on the rims of glasses. Do like the pros in cocktail bars!

The simplest thing is to place the fruit, such as a sprig of currants or a slice of kiwi or pineapple, right on the rim of the glass.

Another fresh idea is to place fruit such as bananas and strawberries on small skewers. Cut the fruit into bite-size pieces and pierce with toothpicks or cocktail skewers.

Citrus peels are also great. Before squeezing out the juice, rinse the fruit under hot water and remove a spiral layer of peel that's as thin as possible.

You can also freeze orange slices to produce a "frosty" garnish that can be floated in the drinks later on. Or freeze fruits such as cherries, blackberries, or raspberries in ice cube trays suspended in a little water or juice.

Drinks look extremely fancy when their rims are coated with sugar or, in the case of vegetable drinks, salt. Dip the rim of the glass in water, lemon juice, or the drink itself to a depth of about 1/4-inch and then dip it in sugar or salt.

MATERIALS

Keep the following on hand:

✗ Measuring cup with a 1/4 to 2-cup scale for measuring liquids.

✗ Long-handled spoon or small wire whisk for stirring.

✗ Toothpicks and wooden skewers for garnishing.

✗ Maraschino cherries for decoration.

✗ Different shaped ice cube trays—for example, hearts, spheres, or stars.

✗ Straws on which you can also skewer fruits such as banana slices.

✗ Punch bowl for larger quantities of drinks.

Eye Appeal

It's best to use a very sharp knife or zesting tool to cut the peel from citrus fruits.

2 Fruity

The fastest way to pep up a drink is with fruit that you set aside during preparation. Depending on the type of fruit, simply hang sprigs on the rim of the glass or cut a slit and wedge it on the rim.

Icy

If you don't want your drinks to be watered down, freeze fruit in juice instead of water.

Healthy Starters

As soon as you get out of bed, load up on fresh vitamins. That will get you operating at full power and increase your energy so you won't lag halfway through the morning. If the night before was a little rough, you'll need as many vitamins as possible, as well as lots and lots of liquids.

Quick Recipes

Blackberry Power Smoothie

SERVES 2:

➤ 1 grapefruit (may substitute ½ cup juice) | ¾ cup blackberries | 1 cup black currant juice | 6 ice cubes | 2 tbs raspberry syrup

1 | Squeeze juice from grapefruit (yields about ½ cup). Rinse blackberries, sort, and drain well.

2 | Combine grapefruit juice, blackberries, half the currant juice, and ice cubes in a blender and purée until the consistency is uniform.

3 | Pour into two tall glasses, top each with remaining currant juice, and add syrup to taste. If desired, serve with ice cubes.

Passion Fruit Kefir

SERVES 2:

➤ 2 oranges (may substitute ⅔ cup juice) 1 peach | 1 cup kefir | ½ cup passion fruit juice (or ¼ cup passion fruit nectar) | 2 tbs honey

1 | Squeeze juice from oranges (yields about ⅔ cup). Pour boiling water over peach, peel, cut in half, and remove pit. Cut off two wedges and set aside for garnish. Dice remaining peach.

2 | Combine orange juice, peach, kefir, passion fruit juice (if using nectar, mix with ¼ cup water), and honey in a blender or whisk well with a hand blender. Pour into two tall glasses. Cut a slit in the two peach wedges and place on rims of glasses.

Invigorating | Creamy

Raspberry Melon Smoothie

SERVES 2:

- 10 oz watermelon
- 1 banana
- $^1/_2$ cup unfiltered apple juice
- 1 pint fresh raspberries (may substitute 8 oz frozen raspberries)
- 3 tbs raspberry syrup
- 1 tbs sugar

Prep time: 10 minutes

Calories per serving: About 210

1 | Scoop flesh of melon from rind, remove dark seeds, and dice fruit. Peel banana and slice.

2 | Combine apple juice, raspberries, 2 tbs raspberry syrup, melon, and banana in a blender and blend at the highest speed until the drink becomes creamy.

3 | Pour remaining raspberry syrup onto a plate. Moisten rims of glasses in syrup, then dip in granulated sugar. Pour drink into glasses.

Mild | Rich in Vitamins

Apricot Buttermilk

SERVES 2:

- $^1/_2$ cantaloupe
- 3–4 apricots
- 1 banana
- $1^1/_4$ cups buttermilk

Prep time: 5 minutes

Calories per serving: About 180

1 | Remove seeds from cantaloupe. Cut off two thin wedges and set aside for garnish. Peel and dice remaining melon. Rinse apricots, cut in half, remove pits, and chop. Peel banana and slice.

2 | Pour buttermilk into a blender or tall measuring cup. Add cantaloupe, apricots, and banana and blend or purée with a hand blender.

3 | Pour buttermilk into two tall glasses. Cut a slit in both saved cantaloupe wedges and place of rims of glasses.

Refreshing | Creamy

Mint Fruit Kefir

SERVES 2:

- 1 pint strawberries
- 1 nectarine
- 2 stalks fresh mint
- 1 cup kefir
- 1 tsp vanilla extract
- 2 tbs sugar
- 4 ice cubes

Prep time: 10 minutes

Calories per serving: About 120

1 | Rinse strawberries, drain well, and remove stems. Rinse nectarine, cut in half, remove pit, and cut into pieces. Remove 5 mint leaves from the stalks.

2 | Combine kefir, vanilla, sugar, ice cubes, fruit, and mint leaves in a blender or tall measuring cup and purée at the highest speed until creamy. Pour into two large glasses and place the two mint stalks in the drinks as garnish.

Sweet | Rich in Vitamins

Caramel Fig Drink

SERVES 2:

- 2 ripe purple figs
  2 large ripe apricots
  1 tsp vanilla extract
  2 tbs sugar
  2 tbs caramel syrup
  1½ cups milk

🕐 Prep time: 5 minutes
- Calories per serving:
  About 210

1 | Rinse figs, pat dry, and cut out cores. Rinse apricots under hot water, cut in half, and remove pits.

2 | Dice fruit. Combine with vanilla, sugar, syrup, and half the milk and purée in a blender or with a hand blender.

3 | Pour drink into two tall glasses and add remaining milk.

Spicy Hot | Creamy

Pepper Strawberry Drink

SERVES 2:

- 1 pint strawberries
  2 nectarines
  1 tbs sugar, as desired
  Freshly ground black pepper
  6–8 ice cubes

🕐 Prep time: 10 minutes
- Calories per serving:
  About 120

1 | Rinse strawberries, remove stems, and cut into quarters or halves. Rinse nectarines under hot water, cut in half, remove pits, and dice fruit.

2 | Combine fruit, sugar (as desired), pepper, and ice cubes in a blender and purée until creamy.

3 | Pour into two tall glasses and grind pepper over the top if desired.

Mild | Perks You Up

Mango Whey Cream

SERVES 2:

- ½ mango (5–6 oz)
  2 ripe apricots
  2 tbs almond butter (optional)
  1 cup pure whey (or 2 tsp powdered whey, available in health food stores, and 1 cup water)
  4 ice cubes
  1 tbs brown sugar

🕐 Prep time: 10 minutes
- Calories per serving:
  About 220

1 | Peel mango and cut away fruit from pit in wedges. Rinse apricots, pat dry, cut in half, remove pits, and chop.

2 | Combine almond butter, whey, chopped fruit, and ice cubes in a blender and purée until creamy.

3 | Spread sugar on a plate, moisten rims of glasses with the Mango Whey Cream, and dip in sugar. Pour drink into glasses and serve with ice cubes if desired.

Invigorating | Creamy
Fruity Pineapple

SERVES 2:

➤ **9 oz fresh pineapple**
  1 nectarine
  1 cup frozen raspberries
  **2 oranges (may substitute
  $^2/_3$ cup orange juice)**
  Sugar, as desired

⏲ Prep time: 10 minutes
➤ Calories per serving:
  About 130

1 | Peel pineapple, remove brown eyes, and cut away from hard center core. Cut off two thin crescents and set aside for garnish. Peel remainder of fruit and dice. Rinse nectarine under hot water, cut in half, remove pit, and dice.

2 | Combine fruit, including raspberries, in a blender or measuring cup. Squeeze juice from oranges and add. Purée drink until the raspberries can no longer be seen.

3 | If desired, sweeten to taste with sugar and pour into two tall glasses. Cut a slit in the pineapple crescents and place on rims of glasses.

Stimulating
For Spooning
Pineapple Vitamin Drink

SERVES 2:

➤ **9 oz fresh pineapple**
  1 banana
  2 oranges
  **1 small bunch red currants
  (see Tip on page 35)**
  2 tsp vanilla extract
  4 tbs sugar
  4 ice cubes
  **Cold mineral water
  (optional)**
  Sugar for garnish

⏲ Prep time: 15 minutes
➤ Calories per serving:
  About 180

1 | Peel pineapple, remove brown eyes and hard center core, and dice. Peel banana and slice. Squeeze juice from oranges. Rinse currants and pluck berries from stems.

2 | Combine fruit, vanilla, and sugar in a blender or tall measuring cup and purée finely. Place ice cubes in two tall glasses and pour drink over the top. If desired, add cold mineral water.

TIP
An easy way to remove those pesky brown eyes left behind on pineapple flesh after peeling is to look for the pattern. You'll notice that they run in a top to bottom diagonal fashion. These can be quickly removed by cutting them out in a wedge all the way around the perimeter. You'll also minimize waste using this method.

Spiced | Invigorating

Tomato Carrot Juice

SERVES 2:

➤ 1 tbs sesame seeds
2 tomatoes
4 sprigs fresh thyme
1 cup carrot juice
3/4 cup kefir
Salt
Worcestershire sauce

🕐 Prep time: 10 minutes
➤ Calories per serving: About 65

1 | In a nonstick pan, toast sesame seeds until golden. Pour boiling water over tomatoes, peel, remove cores, and dice. Remove thyme leaves from stems.

2 | Finely purée tomatoes, thyme, and carrot juice. Whisk in kefir. Season to taste with salt and Worcestershire sauce.

3 | Moisten rims of glasses with juice and dip in sesame seeds, then pour drink into glasses.

Spicy Hot | Invigorating

Kiwi Cucumber Mixer

SERVES 2:

➤ 1 cucumber
2 kiwifruit
1 tbs freshly chopped basil
1 1/4 cups soy milk
Freshly ground pepper
Tabasco, as desired

🕐 Prep time: 10 minutes
➤ Calories per serving: About 80

1 | Peel cucumber and dice finely. Cut kiwifruit in half and scrape out flesh with a spoon.

2 | Combine cucumber, kiwi, basil, and soy milk in a blender and purée finely. Season with pepper and Tabasco and pour into two tall glasses.

TIP You can also prepare this drink with regular milk but then you'll need to drink it quickly because the enzymes in the kiwi turn milk bitter.

Spicy Hot | Hearty

Red Kefir

SERVES 2:

➤ 2/3 cup beet juice
1 tsp grated horseradish (from a jar)
1 1/4 cups kefir
Freshly ground black pepper
Ground coriander
10 chives

🕐 Prep time: 5 minutes
➤ Calories per serving: About 50

1 | Whisk together beet juice and horseradish thoroughly. Vigorously stir in kefir until creamy. Season to taste with pepper and coriander.

2 | Pour drink into two tall glasses and garnish with 5 chive spears.

Light Snacks

Are you feeling a little hungry but you're already overspent on your calorie budget? A light vegetable or fruit drink, enjoyed in small sips, can quickly give your mind and body what they need. You might even replace a meal with one of these low-cal beverages.

Quick Recipes

Yogurt Mint Shake

SERVES 2:

> 2 pink grapefruit (may substitute
> ³/₄ cup juice) | 2 stalks fresh mint |
> 1¹/₄ cups yogurt | 2 tbs honey

1 | Squeeze juice from grapefruit. Rinse
mint sprigs and shake thoroughly dry.
Remove 10 leaves from lower end of stalks
and chop coarsely. Set aside remaining
mint stalks for garnish.

2 | Combine grapefruit juice, mint, yogurt,
and honey in a blender or use a hand
blender and mix until creamy. Pour into
two large glasses. Serve garnished with
mint stalks or leaves.

Cherry Banana Mixer

SERVES 2:

> 1 banana | 2 oranges | 1 cup cherry
> juice | Ice cubes | 6 cherries |
> Wooden skewers (for garnish)

1 | Peel banana and slice. If desired, set
aside several slices for garnish. Squeeze
juice from oranges.

2 | Combine bananas, orange juice,
cherry juice, and ice cubes and purée in
a blender until ice has turned into fine
crystals and the drink is creamy. Pour into
two large glasses. Alternate banana slices
and cherries on wooden skewers and lay
across rims of glasses.

Refreshing | Creamy

Raspberry Smoothie

SERVES 2:

➤ 1 cup frozen raspberries
3 ripe apricots
2 tbs raspberry syrup
$1/2$ tsp cinnamon
$2/3$ cup ice-cold mineral water

🕐 Prep time: 5 minutes
➤ Calories per serving: About 105

1 | Place frozen raspberries in a blender. Rinse apricots under hot water, cut in half, remove pits, and dice. Add apricots to blender.

2 | Pour raspberry syrup over fruit. Add cinnamon and a little water. Blend at the highest speed for 2–3 minutes until creamy.

3 | Pour into two large glasses and thin with ice-cold mineral water as desired.

Tart | Fizzy

Strawberry Balsamic

SERVES 2:

➤ $1^{1}/_{2}$ cups ripe strawberries
2 sprigs basil
1 tbs honey
1 tbs balsamic vinegar
8 ice cubes
$1/2$ cup ice-cold mineral water
Freshly ground black pepper

🕐 Prep time: 10 minutes
➤ Calories per serving: About 70

1 | Rinse strawberries, drain well, remove stems, and cut into halves or quarters. Remove lower leaves from basil sprigs and cut into strips.

2 | Combine strawberries, basil, honey, balsamic vinegar, ice cubes, and a little mineral water in a blender and beat until creamy.

3 | Pour into two large glasses, grind pepper over the top, and serve garnished with basil sprigs or leaves.

Fruity | Exotic

Coconut Strawberry Drink

SERVES 2:

➤ 1 cup strawberries
2 nectarines
3 tbs grated coconut
2 tbs powdered sugar
$1^{1}/_{4}$ cups milk

🕐 Prep time: 10 minutes
➤ Calories per serving: About 280

1 | Carefully rinse strawberries, remove stems, and cut into halves or quarters. Rinse nectarines under hot water, cut in half, remove pits, and dice.

2 | Combine fruit, 2 tbs grated coconut, powdered sugar, and milk and purée finely in a blender or with a hand blender.

3 | Moisten rims of glasses with water. Spread remaining grated coconut on a plate and press rims of glasses into coconut so that it sticks. Pour in drinks and serve sprinkled with remaining coconut.

Refreshing | Spicy Hot
Green Soy Milk

SERVES 2:

- 2 kiwifruit

  2 tbs lemon juice

  2 tbs chopped herbs (parsley, dill, watercress, chervil, chives)

  2 tbs yeast flakes (health food store)

  1¼ cups soy milk

  2 dashes Worcestershire sauce

  Salt | Freshly ground pepper

  Cucumber (for garnish)

- Prep time: 10 minutes
- Calories per serving: About 90

1 | Peel kiwifruit, quarter lengthwise, and dice.

2 | Combine kiwifruit, lemon juice, herbs, yeast flakes, and soy milk and purée finely in a blender.

3 | Spice to taste with Worcestershire sauce, salt, and pepper and pour into two large glasses. Cut cucumber lengthwise and make several slits in each piece, leaving the cucumber attached at the end. Fan out cucumber leaves and place in glasses.

Mild | Spiced
Thyme Cucumber Mixer

SERVES 2:

- 1 cucumber

  ¼ honeydew melon

  ¾ cup buttermilk

  1 tbs chopped thyme

  2 tbs lime juice

  Salt

  Freshly ground pepper

  2 thyme sprigs (for garnish)

- Prep time: 10 minutes
- Calories per serving: About 85

1 | Peel cucumber and dice. Remove seeds from honeydew, peel, and chop.

2 | Combine cucumber, melon, buttermilk, thyme, and lime juice and purée until creamy in a blender or with a hand blender.

3 | Season to taste with salt and pepper and pour into two glasses. Garnish each drink with a thyme sprig.

Spicy Hot | Tart
Cranberry Orange Drink

SERVES 2:

- 2 oranges

  ¼ cup cranberries

  1 tsp sugar

  1 tsp grated horseradish (from a jar)

  1½ cups buttermilk

  Salt

- Prep time: 5 minutes
- Calories per serving: About 95

1 | Cut two wedges from oranges and set aside for garnish. Squeeze juice from remaining oranges. Purée finely with cranberries, sugar, and horseradish.

2 | Thoroughly whisk together orange-cranberry purée and buttermilk and season to taste with salt. Cut a slit in saved orange wedges and place them over the rim of the glass.

TIP If you like it hot, season to taste with more horseradish or Tabasco.

Hearty | Invigorating

Tomato Buttermilk with Cress

SERVES 2:

- 1 cucumber
  1 small bunch watercress
  1 cup tomato juice
  1 cup buttermilk
  Salt
  Freshly ground pepper
  Freshly grated nutmeg

⏱ Prep time: 10 minutes
- Calories per serving:
  About 60

1 | Peel cucumber and dice. Rinse watercress, drain well, and remove any thick stems.

2 | Combine cucumber, two-thirds of the watercress, tomato juice, and half the buttermilk in a blender or tall measuring cup and purée finely.

3 | Season to taste with salt, pepper, and nutmeg and pour into two large glasses. Add remaining buttermilk and serve sprinkled with remaining watercress.

Mild | Perks You Up

Summer Buttermilk

SERVES 2:

- 1 grapefruit
  $3/4$ cup carrot juice
  1 pinch freshly grated nutmeg
  $1 1/4$ cups buttermilk
  Salt or 2 tbs honey, as desired

⏱ Prep time: 5 minutes
- Calories per serving:
  About 50

1 | Squeeze juice from grapefruit and pour through a strainer if desired. Whisk together thoroughly with carrot juice, nutmeg, and buttermilk.

2 | Spice up with salt or sweeten with honey to taste, depending on your preference. Carrots and buttermilk taste delicious either sweet or salty.

Creamy | Spicy Hot

Radish Milk

SERVES 2:

- 12 radishes (about 7 oz)
  $1 1/2$ cups buttermilk
  $3/4$ cup beet juice
  Salt
  Freshly ground pepper
  Worcestershire sauce, as desired

⏱ Prep time: 10 minutes
- Calories per serving:
  About 55

1 | Rinse radishes thoroughly, clean, and dice finely.

2 | Combine radishes and $3/4$ cup buttermilk in a blender or tall measuring cup and purée until creamy. Add remaining buttermilk and blend a little more.

3 | Season to taste with salt, pepper, and Worcestershire sauce. Pour into two tall glasses, add beet juice, and stir briefly with a long-handled spoon.

Mild | Creamy

Soy Avocado Drink

SERVES 2:

- 1 tbs pine nuts
  $1/2$ ripe avocado
  1 kiwifruit
  2 tbs lime juice
  $1^1/2$ cups soy milk
  Freshly ground black pepper

🕐 Prep time: 15 minutes

➤ Calories per serving: About 225

1 | Chop pine nuts coarsely and toast in a nonstick pan until golden.

2 | Remove avocado pit and scrape out flesh with a spoon. Cut kiwifruit in half, cut off two slices for garnish, peel rest of fruit, and dice.

3 | Combine pine nuts, avocado, kiwi, lime juice, and half the soy milk and purée finely in a blender or with a hand blender.

4 | Season to taste with pepper and pour into two tall glasses. Add remaining soy milk and stir with a long-handled spoon. Cut a slit in saved kiwifruit slices and garnish over the rim of each glass.

Hearty | Rich in Vitamins

Avocado Carrot Mixer

SERVES 2:

- $1/2$ ripe avocado
  1 piece fresh ginger (about 1-inch in diameter)
  $1/2$ cup yogurt
  $1^1/4$ cups carrot juice
  $3/4$ cup milk

🕐 Prep time: 10 minutes

➤ Calories per serving: About 230

1 | Remove avocado pit and scrape out flesh with a spoon. Peel ginger and squeeze through a garlic press.

2 | Finely purée avocado, ginger, and yogurt and mix with carrot juice.

3 | Pour Avocado Carrot Mixer into two tall glasses and fold in milk.

TIP

Avocado Basil Drink

For another sophisticated drink with an avocado base, you'll need 1 large bunch basil, 2 tbs lemon juice, $1/2$ ripe avocado, $1^1/2$ cups buttermilk, 1 tsp mustard, and freshly ground black pepper. Rinse basil, pull off leaves, and purée in a blender with lemon juice, avocado flesh, and buttermilk. Spice up slightly with mustard to taste, pour into two tall glasses, and serve dusted with pepper.

For Relaxation and Pleasure

It's finally quitting time! The weekend is here at last! All you want to do is indulge your body and soul. So relax with creamy, flavorful drinks that melt on your tongue and pamper your taste buds.

Quick Recipes

Orange Creamsicle

SERVES 2:

> 3 nectarines | 2 oranges | 10 cherries
> 3 tbs powdered sugar | 6–8 ice cubes

2 | Rinse nectarines under hot water, cut in half, remove pits, and dice. Squeeze juice from oranges. Remove stems and pits from cherries.

2 | Combine fruit, powdered sugar, and ice cubes in a blender and purée until creamy. Pour into two tall glasses and serve immediately.

TIP This drink is especially refreshing if you refrigerate the fruit beforehand.

Chestnut Yogurt

SERVES 2:

> $^3/_4$ cup chestnuts (canned) |
> $^3/_4$ cup yogurt stirred until creamy |
> 2 tbs caramel syrup (may substitute powdered sugar) | 1 cup milk |
> 4 ice cubes | Cinnamon for dusting

1 | Pour chestnuts into a sieve and drain well. Chop chestnuts roughly with a sharp knife. With a hand blender, finely purée chestnuts, yogurt, and syrup. Gradually add milk until the drink is creamy.

2 | Place ice cubes in two large glasses and pour chestnut yogurt over the top. Dust with cinnamon and serve immediately.

31

Refreshing | Light

Vanilla Buttermilk Float

SERVES 2:

- 1 ripe nectarine
- 1 ripe apricot
- 1 tsp vanilla extract
- 2 tbs sugar
- 1 tbs lemon juice
- 2 cups buttermilk
- 2 large scoops vanilla ice cream
- Cinnamon (optional)

🕐 Prep time: 10 minutes

➤ Calories per serving: About 165

1 | Peel nectarine, cut in half, and remove pit. Rinse apricots and remove pits. Chop fruit.

2 | Purée fruit, vanilla, sugar, and lemon juice with a little buttermilk. Stir in remaining buttermilk.

3 | Place ice cream scoops in two large glasses and pour fruit buttermilk over the top. If desired, serve sprinkled with cinnamon.

Velvety | Invigorating

Blackberry Cream

SERVES 2:

- 1 cup blackberries
- 1 cup kefir
- 3/4 cup elderberry juice (may substitute cranberry juice)
- 1/2 tsp cinnamon
- 1/2 cup whipping cream
- 2 tsp powdered sugar
- 2 long cinnamon sticks

🕐 Prep time: 10 minutes

➤ Calories per serving: About 270

1 | Rinse blackberries, sort, and drain well. Combine with kefir, elderberry juice, and half the cinnamon and purée until creamy in a blender or with a hand blender.

2 | Whip cream until stiff, add powdered sugar, and whip 1–2 more minutes.

3 | Pour blackberry drink into two large glasses, top with cream, and sprinkle with remaining cinnamon. Insert cinnamon sticks as garnish.

Fruity | Bubbly

Strawberry Kefir

SERVES 2:

- 1 cup strawberries
- 1 cup blueberries
- 1 cup kefir
- 2 tsp almond butter
- 1 tsp vanilla extract
- 2 tbs sugar
- Mineral water, as desired

🕐 Prep time: 15 minutes

➤ Calories per serving: About 165

1 | Rinse strawberries, drain, remove stems, and cut in half. Rinse and sort blueberries.

2 | Combine fruit, kefir, almond butter, vanilla, and sugar, and purée until creamy in a blender or with a hand blender.

3 | Pour into two tall glasses and add mineral water as desired.

For Spooning
Buttermilk Pears

SERVES 2:

➤ **2 small ripe pears (about 8 oz)**
$2/3$ cup white or red currants (see Tip)
$1 1/2$ cups buttermilk
3 tbs sugar
1 tsp cinnamon

🕐 Prep time: 10 minutes
➤ Calories per serving: About 150

TIP

Mixed Berries
You can easily use other types of berries in place of currants. All currant drinks taste great with fresh, aromatic strawberries, fresh or frozen raspberries, or blueberries. You can also use a prepared berry mixture (available frozen) to make a fruity, refreshing drink.

1 | Peel pears, cut into quarters, remove cores, and cut up fruit. Rinse currants, drain well, and pluck from stems.

2 | Combine buttermilk, sugar, and $1/2$ tsp cinnamon in a blender or tall measuring cup, add fruit, and blend at high speed until creamy.

3 | Pour into two tall glasses and serve sprinkled with remaining cinnamon.

Smooth | Bubbly
Nectarine Smoothie

SERVES 2:

➤ **2 tbs sliced almonds**
1 small banana
1 nectarine
3 ice-cold oranges (may substitute $3/4$ cup juice)
1 tbs honey
4 ice cubes
$3/4$ cup ice-cold mineral water, as desired

🕐 Prep time: 15 minutes
➤ Calories per serving: About 140

1 | In a nonstick pan, toast sliced almonds until golden and let cool.

2 | Peel banana and cut into slices $1/2$ inch thick. Cut nectarine in half, remove pit, and dice. Squeeze juice from oranges.

3 | Combine orange juice, sliced almonds, honey, fruit, and ice cubes in a blender and purée until creamy.

4 | Pour into two tall glasses and add ice-cold mineral water as desired.

Smooth | Exotic

Mango Ginger Smoothie

SERVES 2:

- ➤ ¹/₂ mango (about 5 oz fruit)
- 1 piece fresh ginger (about walnut-sized)
- 4 oranges
- 1 lime
- 6 ice cubes

🕐 Prep time: 10 minutes

➤ Calories per serving: About 90

1 | Peel mango, cut away fruit from hard pit, and dice. Peel ginger and squeeze through a garlic press.

2 | Cut oranges in half and cut two slices from the middle for garnish. Squeeze juice from oranges and lime.

3 | Combine mango, ginger, orange juice, lime juice, and ice cubes in a blender and blend until creamy.

4 | Pour into two large glasses. Cut slits in orange slices and place on rims of glasses.

Creamy | Exotic

Fig Milk

SERVES 2:

- ➤ 2 tbs shelled pistachios
- 3 fresh dark figs
- 1¹/₄ cups milk
- ¹/₂ cup yogurt, drained
- 1 tbs honey
- ¹/₂ tsp ground cardamom
- 4 ice cubes
- ¹/₃ cup whipping cream (optional)
- 1 tsp sugar

🕐 Prep time: 15 minutes

➤ Calories per serving: About 260

1 | In a nonstick pan, toast pistachios until golden. Cut two slices from the center of one fig for garnish. Dice remaining figs, combine with pistachios and ¹/₂ cup milk, and purée finely.

2 | Add remaining milk, yogurt, honey, and cardamom and stir well.

3 | Place ice cubes in two large glasses and pour Fig Milk over the top. If desired, whip cream until partially or completely stiff and place on top.

4 | Spread sugar on a plate. Moisten fig slices slightly, press into sugar and place on rims of glasses.

Summer Party

Non-alcoholic is "in." Headaches are out. These light, ice-cold beverages are sure to be the hit of any summer party and a snap to mix. If you don't want them to be entirely "virgin," add some sparkling wine to your drinks and punches.

Quick Recipes

Pink Bananas

SERVES 2:

➤ 1 small banana | 1 tbs raspberry syrup |
1 tbs honey | 1^1/$_2$ cups milk |
^{1}/$_4$ cup whipping cream (optional)

1 | Peel banana and slice. Set aside two
slices for garnish. Combine banana,
raspberry syrup, honey, and 1 cup milk in
a blender or tall measuring cup and purée.

2 | Pour into two tall glasses and add
remaining milk.

3 | If desired, whip cream and use to top
drink. Serve garnished with banana slices.

Blue Coconut

SERVES 2:

➤ 4 oranges | 2 tbs non-alcoholic curacao
or orange syrup | 2 tbs coconut syrup
(may substitute ^{1}/$_4$ cup coconut milk) |
4 ice cubes | 1 cup pineapple juice |
Ice-cold mineral water

1 | Cut oranges in half and cut two slices
from the middle to use as garnish. Squeeze
remaining oranges (should yield about
1 cup). Thoroughly whisk together juice
and two types of syrup.

2 | Place ice cubes in two large glasses,
pour orange syrup mixture over the
top, and add pineapple juice.

3 | Add ice-cold mineral water as desired
and garnish with orange slices.

Creamy | Sweet

Apple Punch

SERVES 2:

- 2 tbs raisins
  2 cups apple juice
  3 ripe purple figs
  2 tbs frozen concentrated apple juice
  4 ice cubes
  Crushed ice (optional)

🕐 Prep time: 10 minutes
🕐 Marinating time: 1 hour
➤ Calories per serving: About 255

1 | Soak raisins in ½ cup apple juice for 1 hour. Rinse figs, pat dry, and remove cores. Dice 1 fig finely and set aside.

2 | Coarsely chop remaining figs. Combine figs, raisins with marinating liquid, frozen and fresh apple juice, and ice cubes in a blender and purée.

3 | Pour into two large glasses (over crushed ice, if desired) and fold in diced fig.

Refreshing | Tart

Pineapple Punch

SERVES 2:

- 1 cup cleaned pineapple flesh
  10 cherries
  2 tbs coconut syrup (may substitute honey)
  ¾ cup bitters (non-alcoholic Italian aperitif)
  ½ cup pineapple juice
  Mineral water and ice cubes as desired

🕐 Prep time: 10 minutes
🕐 Marinating time: 1 hour
➤ Calories per serving: About 150

1 | Cut pineapple into small pieces. Cut cherries in half and remove pits. Place fruit in a bowl and pour syrup on top.

2 | Add bitters until fruit is completely covered. Marinate in the refrigerator for at least 1 hour.

3 | Pour into two large glasses and add remaining bitters and pineapple juice. Thin with mineral water and add ice cubes as desired.

Fizzy | Tart

Iced Melon

SERVES 2:

- ¼ honeydew melon (about 8 oz fruit)
  1 piece fresh ginger (about 1 inch in diameter)
  2 tbs honey
  1 tsp finely chopped lemon zest
  4 ice cubes or crushed ice (see page 6)
  1 cup tonic water

🕐 Prep time: 10 minutes
🕐 Marinating time: 1 hour
➤ Calories per serving: About 120

1 | Remove seeds from honeydew, peel, and dice. Peel ginger and squeeze through a garlic press.

2 | Combine melon, ginger, honey, and lemon zest in a bowl and marinate in the refrigerator for 1 hour.

3 | Purée fruit coarsely with a hand blender. In two large glasses, pour over ice cubes or crushed ice and add tonic water.

Refreshing | Tart
Nectarine Tea

SERVES 2:

- 2 teabags rosehip tea
  2 nectarines
  2 tsp finely chopped lemon zest
  3 tbs passion fruit syrup (may substitute honey)
  6 ice cubes
  Mint sprigs

- Prep time: 10 minutes, not including refrigeration time
- Calories per serving: About 50

1 | Steep rosehip tea according to package directions in at least 1 cup boiling water and let stand. Chill in refrigerator until cold.

2 | Rinse nectarines, cut in half, remove pits, and dice.

3 | Combine nectarines, lemon zest, syrup, ice cubes, and half the rosehip tea in a blender and purée until creamy. Pour into two glasses and add remaining tea. Garnish with mint.

Light | Rich in Vitamins
Orange Rosehip Punch

SERVES 2:

- 2 teabags rosehip tea
  2 oranges
  1 lemon
  2 ripe peaches

- Prep time: 10 minutes, not including refrigeration time
- Calories per serving: About 75

1 | Prepare tea with at least 1¼ cups boiling water and chill in refrigerator until cold. Cut two thin slices from the center of one orange and place in the freezer.

2 | Squeeze juice from oranges and lemon. Peel peaches, cut in half, and remove pits. Finely dice half of one peach. Cut up remaining peaches, purée along with orange juice, lemon juice, and a little tea and then add remaining tea.

3 | Place frozen orange slices and diced peach in glasses and pour punch over top.

Sweet | Invigorating
Apricot Tea

SERVES 2:

- 1 teabag green tea
  6 ripe apricots
  2 oranges (may substitute ²⁄₃ cup orange juice)
  2 tbs grenadine syrup
  4 ice cubes

- Prep time: 10 minutes, not including refrigeration time
- Calories per serving: About 125

1 | Prepare green tea according to package directions with at least 1 cup water and let stand. Chill in refrigerator until cold.

2 | Rinse apricots under hot water, cut in half, remove pits, and dice coarsely. Squeeze juice from oranges.

3 | Combine apricots, orange juice, syrup, ice cubes, and one half of the green tea in a blender or tall measuring cup and purée.

4 | Pour into two large glasses and add remaining tea. Add more ice cubes as desired.

Creamy | Exotic
Virgin Piña Colada

SERVES 2:

- 1/2 cup yogurt, drained
- 3 tbs coconut syrup (may substitute 1/4 cup coconut milk)
- 2 cups pineapple juice
- Crushed ice (see page 6)
- 1 slice pineapple (fresh or canned)
- 2 maraschino cherries

Prep time: 10 minutes

- Calories per serving: About 140

1 | Stir together yogurt and coconut syrup until smooth. Add part of pineapple juice and continue stirring. Add remaining pineapple juice.

2 | Fill two large glasses two-thirds full with ice and pour drink over the top.

3 | Cut pineapple slice in half. With toothpicks, attach a maraschino cherry to each slice and lay on top of glasses.

Fruity | Refreshing
Kiwi Colada

SERVES 2:

- 3 kiwifruit
- 3/4 cup cherry juice
- 4 ice cubes or crushed ice (see page 6)
- 3/4 cup pear juice
- Ice-cold mineral water, as desired
- 2 maraschino cherries (optional)

Prep time: 10 minutes

- Calories per serving: About 120

1 | Peel kiwifruit. From 1 kiwi, cut 4 slices crosswise from the center and set aside for garnish. Quarter remaining kiwi lengthwise and remove hard white core.

2 | Purée kiwifruit and cherry juice. In two chilled glasses, pour over ice. Add pear juice and thin with mineral water.

3 | If desired, combine kiwi slices and maraschino cherries on wooden skewers and place in glasses as garnish.

Invigorating | Tart
Peach Tonic

SERVES 2:

- 1 ripe white peach
- 1 lemon
- 3 tbs kiwifruit nectar (may substitute peach nectar)
- 1 1/2 cups tonic water
- 1 tbs sugar
- 4 ice cubes

Prep time: 10 minutes

- Calories per serving: About 110

1 | Pour boiling water over peach, peel, remove pit, and chop. Squeeze juice from lemon.

2 | Combine chopped peach, lemon juice, 2 tbs kiwifruit nectar, and 1/2 cup tonic water and purée.

3 | Spread remaining nectar and sugar on two separate, small plates. Moisten rims of glasses with kiwi nectar and then dip in sugar.

4 | Place ice cubes in glasses, pour peach cream over the top, and add remaining tonic water.

Sweet | Relaxing

Apricot Cooler

SERVES 2:

➤ 3 ripe apricots
2 tbs banana syrup
(may substitute honey)
$1/2$ lemon
$1^1/2$ cups unfiltered
apple juice
4 ice cubes

🕐 Prep time: 10 minutes
➤ Calories per serving:
About 195

1 | Rinse apricots under hot water, pat dry, cut in half, remove pits, and chop. Combine apricots, banana syrup, juice from lemon, half the apple juice, and ice cubes in a blender and purée finely.

2 | Pour into two large glasses and add remaining apple juice. Add additional ice cubes if desired.

TIP For garnish, you can place apricot pieces and banana slices on toothpicks and lay them across the rims of the glasses.

Tangy | Fizzy

Ginger Pears

SERVES 2:

➤ 2 soft ripe pears
2 tbs pear juice (may
substitute 1 tsp honey)
$1^1/2$ cups ice-cold
ginger ale
2 stalks fresh mint
4 ice cubes

🕐 Prep time: 10 minutes
➤ Calories per serving:
About 315

1 | Peel pears, cut lengthwise into quarters, and remove cores. Chop pears, combine with pear juice and half the ginger ale, and purée.

2 | Rinse mint under cold water, shake thoroughly dry, and place in two large glasses along with ice cubes.

3 | Pour pear purée over ice and add remaining ginger ale.

Fizzy | Tart

Bitter Carambola

SERVES 2:

➤ 1 carambola (star fruit)
1 pink grapefruit
$1/2$ tsp allspice
$1^1/2$ cups bitters
1 lemon
2 tbs frozen concentrated
apple juice, as desired

🕐 Prep time: 10 minutes, not
including marinating time
➤ Calories per serving:
About 145

1 | Cut carambola in half crosswise and set aside two slices from the center for garnish. Dice remaining fruit finely. Squeeze juice from grapefruit and pour through a strainer if desired to make it clear.

2 | Combine diced carambola, grapefruit juice, and allspice, cover, and marinate in the refrigerator for at least 1 hour.

3 | Pour into two large glasses and add bitters and juice from $1/2$ lemon to each glass. Sweeten to taste with concentrated apple juice. Garnish with carambola slices.

Hot Drinks for Cold Days

These mulled drinks warm your body and soul, all at once. Some taste like mulled wine but don't contain a drop of alcohol. Not only that, but they're super healthy! No winter ailments will come anywhere near you.

Quick Recipes

Peanut Milk

SERVES 2:

> 1 piece fresh ginger (about 1 inch in
> diameter) | 2 cups milk | 3 tbs peanut
> butter | Salt | Freshly ground pepper

1 | Peel ginger, squeeze through a garlic
press, and add to milk.

2 | Bring ginger milk to a boil and stir
in peanut butter vigorously using a
wire whisk.

3 | Pour into two tall punch glasses and
season to taste with salt and pepper.

Chocolate Cream

SERVES 2:

> 2 cups milk | 2 tbs chocolate sauce or
> syrup | 1 tsp vanilla extract | 2 tbs
> sugar | $1/3$ cup whipping cream |
> 2 tsp chocolate sprinkles |
> Cinnamon for dusting

1 | Bring milk to a boil and stir in
chocolate sauce, vanilla, and sugar.

2 | Whip cream until very stiff.

3 | Pour hot chocolate drink into two
large glasses or mugs and top with cream.
Garnish with chocolate sprinkles and
cinnamon and serve immediately.

Mild | Invigorating

Hot Mint

SERVES 2:

- **2 cups milk**
- **3 sprigs fresh mint**
- **10 chocolate dinner mints (e.g. After Eight)**
- **1 tbs sugar, as desired**
- **$\frac{1}{2}$ cup whipping cream**
- **2 tsp grated milk chocolate**

🕐 Prep time: 10 minutes

➤ Calories per serving: About 510

1 | Bring milk and 1 sprig mint to a boil. Stir in chocolate mints with a wire whisk. Add a little sugar to taste, if desired.

2 | Place one sprig mint in each of two large martini glasses and pour hot mint milk over the top.

3 | Whip cream until stiff and use to top drinks. Serve sprinkled with grated chocolate.

TIP

Hot Spicy Chocolate

Chocolate doesn't just go with mint. You can also combine thyme with semi-sweet chocolate (also with nougat filling, if desired). Slowly heat 2 cups milk with 1 sprig thyme. Melt 1 cup chocolate into milk and sweeten with sugar if desired. Place 1 sprig thyme in each of two large cups or mugs and pour hot chocolate over the top. Here, too, topping it with whipped cream can't hurt!

Fruity | Velvety

Hot Plums

SERVES 2:

- **2 plums**
- **1 cinnamon stick**
- **2 cups plum juice**
- **1 tsp vanilla extract**
- **2 tbs sugar**
- **$\frac{1}{2}$ tsp allspice**
- **2 tbs lemon juice**

🕐 Prep time: 15 minutes, not including marinating time

➤ Calories per serving: About 235

1 | Cut plums in half, remove pit, and cut into narrow strips. Place in a small bowl with cinnamon stick. Pour boiling water over the top and marinate for 4 hours.

2 | Combine plum juice, vanilla, sugar, and allspice and bring to a boil. Remove cinnamon stick from soaked plums. Purée plums and add to plum juice pot while whisking until foamy.

3 | Add lemon juice to taste and serve hot in pre-warmed glasses.

◀ *Photo top:* **Hot Mint**   *Photo bottom:* **Hot Plums**

Sweet | Invigorating
Orange Punch

SERVES 2:

- ➤ **2 tbs orange pekoe tea**
- **3 oranges**
- **2 whole cloves**
- **1 star anise**
- **2 tbs sugar**
- **2 rock candy sticks for stirring**

🕐 Prep time: 15 minutes
Calories per serving: About 110

1 | Pour 1½ cups boiling water over tea leaves and steep for 5 minutes. Rinse 1 orange under hot water and peel away a very thin spiral strip of rind using a sharp knife or vegetable peeler. Cut spiral in half and place each piece in a large punch glass.

2 | Squeeze juice from oranges. Combine juice, cloves, star anise, and sugar and heat to just below the boiling point. Heat for 5 minutes over low heat but don't let it boil.

3 | Pour tea and spiced orange juice through a strainer onto the orange peels. Immediately serve hot with rock candy sticks.

Sweet | Relaxing
Elderberry Punch

SERVES 2:

- ➤ **1 cup elderberry juice (may substitute cranberry juice)**
- **1 cup unfiltered apple juice**
- **2 tbs pear juice (may substitute 1 tsp honey)**
- **1 cinnamon stick**
- **3 whole cloves**
- **1 piece orange zest**
- **½ vanilla bean**
- **1 tbs honey**

🕐 Prep time: 15 minutes
➤ Calories per serving: About 180

1 | Combine elderberry juice and apple juice in a small, tall-sided pot. Stir in pear juice and add cinnamon stick, cloves, and orange zest.

2 | Slit open vanilla bean lengthwise, scrape out seeds, and add bean and seeds to juice. Bring to a boil, remove from heat, cover, and let stand for 5 minutes.

3 | Pour through a strainer into two large punch glasses and immediately serve hot.

Creamy | Smooth
Virgin Eggnog

SERVES 2:

➤ 2 tbs loose black tea
  1 orange
  2 egg yolks
  3 tbs sugar
  1 tsp vanilla extract

🕐 Prep time: 20 minutes
➤ Calories per serving:
  About 135

1 | Pour 1½ cups boiling water over tea and steep for 10 minutes. Squeeze juice from orange. In a hot double boiler, beat egg yolk, sugar, and vanilla constantly with a wire whisk until foamy.

2 | Add orange juice and continue beating until mixture is foamy.

3 | Remove leaves from tea and gradually add tea to pot and serve almost boiling in large, pre-warmed punch glasses.

Invigorating | Aromatic
Coconut Coffee

SERVES 2:

➤ 2 tbs coconut syrup
  (may substitute ¼ cup
  coconut milk)
  1½ cups strong, hot,
  freshly brewed coffee
  2 tbs brown sugar
  ½ cup whipping cream
  2 tsp grated coconut
  ½ tsp cinnamon

🕐 Prep time: 10 minutes
➤ Calories per serving:
  About 240

1 | Stir coconut syrup into coffee and sweeten to taste with sugar. Pour into two large glasses.

2 | Whip cream until stiff and use to top drink – if desired, use a pastry bag with a star tip.

3 | Combine grated coconut and cinnamon and sprinkle on cream. Immediately serve hot.

TIP Before pouring in the drink, coat the rims of the glasses with powdered sugar and cinnamon.

Sweet | Sour
Mulled Apple

SERVES 2:

➤ 1 tart apple
  1½ cups apple juice
  2 tbs raisins
  1 tbs sugar
  3 whole cloves
  1 cinnamon stick
  1 lemon

🕐 Prep time: 15 minutes
➤ Calories per serving:
  About 200

1 | Rinse apple, remove core, and dice finely.

2 | Combine apple juice, raisins, sugar, cloves, and cinnamon stick in a pot, bring to a boil, and then simmer over low heat for 5 minutes.

3 | Remove cloves and cinnamon stick and purée remaining ingredients coarsely with a hand blender so that a few pieces of apple remain. Squeeze juice from lemon, stir into mixture, and pour into two tall punch glasses.

Revitalizing | Fruity

Rosehip Punch

SERVES 2:

- 2 whole cloves
  2 teabags rosehip tea
  ³/₄ cup frozen raspberries
  ¹/₂ cup black
  currant juice
  2 tsp sugar
  2 pinches cinnamon
  2 cinnamon sticks

- Prep time: 15 minutes
- Calories per serving:
  About 50

1 | Bring 1¼ cups water to a boil with whole cloves, add tea, and steep for 5 minutes.

2 | Remove cloves and teabags. Add raspberries, heat slowly until they thaw, and then purée. Add black currant juice and heat to just below the boiling point. Add sugar to taste.

3 | Pour into two large punch glasses, sprinkle with cinnamon, and insert cinnamon sticks as garnish.

Perks You Up | Fruity

Orange Coffee

SERVES 2:

- 1 orange
  6 whole cloves
  3 tbs brown sugar
  1¼ cups strong hot coffee
  ¹/₂ cup whipping cream

- Prep time: 15 minutes
- Calories per serving:
  About 215

1 | Rinse orange under hot water, dry, and grate off 1 tsp of the zest. Cut two thick slices from the center. Squeeze juice from rest of orange.

2 | Pierce orange slices with cloves and place in a small, high-sided pot with sugar. Heat until sugar begins melting and then add orange juice. Boil for 3 minutes until liquid has thickened slightly. Add coffee and pour into 2 punch glasses.

3 | Whip cream until stiff, place on top of coffee, and serve immediately sprinkled with orange zest.

TIP

Flavoring Coffee

It's so easy to give your coffee a variety of flavors. You can either add spices such as cinnamon, cardamom, or cloves, or alter the taste with a shot of syrup (for example, caramel-flavored).

Glossary

Apricots: Because they're high in potassium, silicic acid, B vitamins, and beta carotene, apricots are a good all-around energy source. They're also considered to be a beauty potion.

Avocados: Avocados are naturally high in polyunsaturated fatty acids and are also rich in biotin, which controls the energy supply to muscles. Biotin is also good for protein metabolism and strengthens hair, nails, and skin. This is why avocados are also considered a beauty fruit.

Bananas: Bananas are super energy boosters and make any drink nice and creamy. Most people simply feel good after eating a banana, because they contain a lot of soothing vitamin B6. Store in a cool place but don't refrigerate.

Berries: Red berries are mainly sources of beta carotene, B vitamins, and vitamin C. They are also high in potassium and calcium. A variety of flavenoids and phenolic acids make berries your body's health brigade. Dark berries also contain anthocyanin, effective protection against cell destruction.

Cherries: Most nutritious in early summer when the fruit is very dark red. These health boosters contain potassium, calcium, iron, magnesium, phosphorus, silicic acid, B vitamins, carotene, and vitamin C.

Citrus fruits: Don't let the sour taste fool you. These fruits can make you fit and healthy. In addition to the obvious vitamin C, these fruits also contain terpene, which is thought to prevent cancer. Pink grapefruit contains lycopene, also contained in tomato juice, which makes both great anti-cancer drinks.

Cloves: Their sweet, lingering aroma spices up punches and warms your cold winter evenings. Will keep for 2 years in a dark, air-tight container.

Cucumbers: Cucumbers aren't just good in salads. Their high water content means they're low in calories and easy to purée. Their relatively neutral flavor also makes them compatible with fruit, such as melons.

Curry, cardamom, and allspice: These spices bring the fragrance of the Middle-East right into your home. Used sparingly, they raise your spirits and improve your mood.

Ginger: This tropical tuberous root has an antiseptic quality and is also good for circulation and digestion. Fresh ginger has a smooth, shiny peel and keeps 2–3 weeks in the vegetable bin of your refrigerator. Sweet fruits take on a hot, spicy tone when you season them with finely grated ginger.

Grapes: Grapes are rich in glucose, which makes them an ideal pick-me-up in the face of mental or physical stress. They taste best during the main harvest time in October. They're loaded with folic acid and iron.

Hazelnuts: Also said to have powers as an aphrodisiac, finely ground hazelnuts can be blended in drinks or sprinkled on top.

Herbs: Parsley, chives, and thyme are great in vegetable drinks. Not only do they add aroma but also provide minerals and essential oils that strengthen the immune system. Mint stalks in a glass not only look nice but also give drinks a fresh flavor.

Mangos and papayas: These are considered the "exotic" fruits but are now available almost everywhere all year round. They're loaded with beta carotene, vitamins, minerals, and enzymes.

Melons: With it's almost 95% water content, watermelon is practically a drink in itself. It's an ideal thirst-quencher in the summer and high in vitamin C. Its sweet relatives (honeydew, cantaloupe, and Galia melon) are excellent for puréeing. Freeze by the serving for ice-cold drinks! When you thump a ripe melon, it sounds hollow.

Peaches and nectarines: These fruits shouldn't be too firm and should have a pleasant fragrance. Make sure they aren't bruised and don't pile them on top of one another! Try sweet white peaches in midsummer— a sensory experience in drinks.

Pears and apples: Easy to digest. Unpeeled, their fiber promotes intestinal peristalsis. Ripe fruit shouldn't be completely hard but should be free of bruises. Make sure the peel is intact. They'll keep in the vegetable bin of your refrigerator for 5–6 days.

Pineapple and kiwi: Excellent sources of vitamin C, especially during the gloomy fall and winter months. Take care though, both contain the protein-digesting enzyme bromelain, which is good for your digestion but turns dairy-products bitter.

Sesame seeds: Contain unsaturated fatty acids and are recommended for preventing arteriosclerosis, high blood pressure, and diabetes. It's best to buy the unhulled or toasted seeds, which are more nutritious. Store in an airtight container.

Syrups: Syrups serve to sweeten and flavor your drinks. You need only one tbs per serving. They're now available in small bottles in well-stocked supermarkets. It's best to start out with one or two kinds of syrup (such as banana and passion fruit) and then if it appeals to you, be more adventurous. Almost any fruit flavor is now available in syrup form.

Tabasco and Worcestershire Sauce: Both liquid seasonings have long been used in cocktail bars. Worcestershire sauce is brewed from countless spices and aged for three years in wooden casks. Both sauces are used by the drop.

Tomatoes: You can process fresh, peeled tomatoes for drinks but in this one case, it's better to buy the prepared juice. Lycopene, the pigment that makes tomatoes red and also protects us from cancer, exercises its properties only after heating.

The Author

Doris Muliar, a native of Salzburg, Austria, has long been living and working in Cologne. After working successfully as a journalist and in the film industry, she made her enthusiasm for cooking and entertaining into a career. She is the author of many books on low-fat nutrition, health, and fitness.

The Photographer

Kai Mewes is an independent food photographer in Munich who works for publishers and in advertising. His studio and test kitchen are located near Munich's famous Viktualienmarkt. His appetizing photos reflect his dedication to combining photography and culinary pleasure. Food styling is the work of Akos Neuberger and Daniel Petri.

Photo Credits

FoodPhotographie Eising, Martina Görlach: cover photo
Stockfood: page 6 (top, bottom center, bottom right); page 7
Teubner: page 6 (bottom left)
All others: Kai Mewes, Munich

Published originally under the title Drinks ohne Alkohol © 2002 Gräfe und Unzer Verlag GmbH, Munich. English translation for the U.S. market © 2003, Silverback Books, Inc.

All rights reserved. No part of this book may be reproduced in any form without the written permission of the publisher.

Food Editor: Jonathan Silverman
Managing editor: Birgit Rademacker
Editor: Stefanie Poziombka
Reader: Elizabeth Penn, Bettina Bartz
Proofreader: Hildegard Toma
Layout, typography and cover design: Independent Medien Design, Munich
Typesetting and production: Patty Holden, Design-Typo-Print, Ismaning, Maike Harmeier

Printed in Korea

ISBN 1-930603-47-9

Enjoy Other Quick & Easy Books

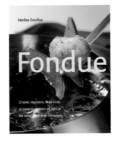

Marlisa Szwillus

Fondue

Cheese, vegetable, or all kinds of meat—prepare them all right at the table. More than 50 recipes.

Cornelia Adam

Salads

An entire cookbook for real appetizers, main dishes, and party dishes. Includes ethnic choices and cutting-edge alternatives.

Sandwiches

Creative snacks bring the fun of international flavor stories. Quick and easy breads and fillings.

Xenia Burgtorf

Cornelia Adam

Quiche

Delicious, select types with vegetables, meat, poultry or fish—some for all occasions.

Cornelia Adam

Garlic

Sophisticated Recipes with the Favorite Spice of the Mediterranean Region. Spicy (tangy), Fine (delicate), international.

Cornelia Schinharl

Easy Vegetarian

Uncomplicated and sophisticated – Vegetarian recipes for all seasons.

Sebastian Dickhaut

Casseroles

The best of everything, sometimes easy, sometimes fine. Recipes for the kitchen.

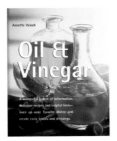

Annette Heisch

Oil & Vinegar

A wonderful source of information, delicious recipes and helpful hints— liven up your favorite dishes and create tasty sauces and dressings.

Andreas Fürtmayr

Sushi

Classic ideas from Japan and new fusion sushi. Home-made perfectly.

1 Noodle, 50 Sauces

Everyday Pasta • Old and New Italian Dishes
Noodle biography • 10 Tips for Success

Healthy Wok

Elisabeth Döpp
Christian Willrich
Joerg Rehbehn

Great for light and satisfying meals

Antje Gruener

Grilling

Crisp, flavorful and spicy vegetable morsels from the grill for your barbecue feast, from appetite to dessert vegetables with sauces and chutneys.

Gina Greifenstein

1 Batter— 50 Cakes

Baking to your heart's content

Cooking in Clay

Healthy Recipes with Great Flavor

Erika Casparek-Türkkan

Doris Muliar

Cocktails for Drivers

100% Enjoyment

Antipasti and Tapas

Mediterranean Appetizers

Cornelia Schinharl

Soups

Classic to Contemporary

Sebastian Dickhaut

Claudia Schmidt

Raclette

New Recipes with Cheese Primer and Party Dips

STANDARD SUPPLIES

> The smart bartender is always prepared and armed, just in case guests show up unexpectedly or someone suddenly wants a fruity drink. You should always have the following on hand: Lots of ice cubes, various frozen fruits (individual or mixed berries), favorite juices, and dairy. You can't go wrong if you have these basics.

Guaranteed Success—
From Milkshakes to Punches

FRESHNESS AND QUALITY OF INGREDIENTS

> These drinks will turn out perfectly if you always purchase first-class ingredients. Buy only undamaged, ripe fruit and vegetables. Fruit in particular must be soft enough to purée easily.

QUICK GARNISH MADE EASY

> The fastest garnish is practically at your fingertips: Simply set aside some part of the fruits or vegetables you used to prepare the drink, then cut a slit in them and set them on the rims of the glasses. Or for spicy drinks, use herbs either in the form of stalks that you stand up in the drink or chopped herbs that you sprinkle on top.

THE RIGHT TEA

> For tea-based mixed drinks, always use a loose, aromatic black tea. Suitable varieties include Assam, orange pekoe, and Ceylon.